An Individual History

ALSO BY MICHAEL COLLIER

The Clasp and Other Poems (1986)

The Folded Heart (1989)

The Neighbor (1995)

The Ledge (2000)

Dark Wild Realm (2006)

TRANSLATION

Medea (2006)

PROSE

Make Us Wave Back: Essays on Poetry and Influence (2007)

EDITIONS

The Wesleyan Tradition: Four Decades of American Poetry (1993)

*The New Bread Loaf Anthology of Contemporary American
Poetry* (with Stanley Plumly) (1999)

The New American Poets: A Bread Loaf Anthology (2000)

A William Maxwell Portrait: Memories and Appreciations (with
Charles Baxter and Edward Hirsch) (2004)

Peter,

Thanks for all of your kind attentions at Gettysburg & for your friendship.

Fondly,

Mike

3/26/13

AN INDIVIDUAL HISTORY · POEMS

Michael Collier

W. W. NORTON & COMPANY

New York · London

For information about permission to reproduce selections from this book,
write to Permissions, W. W. Norton & Company, Inc., 500 Fifth Avenue,
New York, NY 10110

For information about special discounts for bulk purchases, please contact
W. W. Norton Special Sales at specialsales@wwnorton.com or 800-233-4830

Manufacturing by The Maple-Vail Book Manufacturing Group
Book design by Dana Sloan
Production manager: Devon Zahn

Library of Congress Cataloging-in-Publication Data

Collier, Michael, 1953–
  An individual history : poems / Michael Collier. — 1st ed.
     p. cm.
  Includes bibliographical references.
  ISBN 978-0-393-08249-4 (hardcover)
  I. Title.
  PS3553.O474645I53 2012
  811'.54—dc23

                        2012006129

W. W. Norton & Company, Inc., 500 Fifth Avenue, New York, N.Y. 10110
www.wwnorton.com

W. W. Norton & Company Ltd., Castle House, 75/76 Wells Street, London
W1T 3QT

1 2 3 4 5 6 7 8 9 0

For Steve Orlen

(1942–2010)

CONTENTS

An Individual History

Piety

Once I had a good church voice
and having been a Knight of the Altar,
I have impeccable church manners.
I know that sounds superior,
but it's not something I brag about,
rather it's a small, inner satisfaction
and nothing like the superiority
the church organist from my childhood parish
displayed when it came time for him,
the last congregant to take communion,
to climb down from his bench,
exit the sacristy, and through the side chapel
gain the main aisle, all the while
his hands flattened together,
like two soft trowels, arms extended,
elbows turned out, and his head
with its grayish, Liberace pompadour,
thrown back, eyes heavenward.
Any of us who served Mass
knew the inside of his mouth—
bobbed tonsils, missing molars,
silver fillings, and the yellowish, veined,
smoker's tongue hanging over the edge
of his lower lip, moist with holy
adhesive and reptilian in its reach.

An Individual History

This was before the time of lithium and Zoloft

before mood stabilizers and anxiolytics

and almost all the psychotropic drugs, but not before Thorazine,

which the suicide O'Laughlin called "handcuffs for the mind."

It was before, during, and after the time of atomic fallout,

Auschwitz, the Nakba, DDT, and you could take water cures,

find solace in quarantines, participate in shunnings,

or stand at Lourdes among the canes and crutches.

It was when the March of Time kept taking off its boots.

Fridays when families prayed the Living Rosary

to neutralize communists with prayer.

When electroshock was electrocution

and hammers recognized the purpose of a nail.

And so, if you were as crazy as my maternal grandmother was then you might make the pilgrimage she did through the wards

of state and private institutions,

and make of your own body a nail for pounding, its head

sunk past quagmires, coups d'etat, and disappearances

and in this way find a place in history

among the detained and unparoled, an individual like her,

though hidden by an epoch of lean notation—"Marked

Parkinsonian tremor," "Chronic paranoid type"—

a time when the animal slowed by its fate

was excited to catch a glimpse of its tail

or feel through her skin the dulled-over joy

when for a moment her hands were still.

In Certain Situations I'm Very Much Against Birdsong

When poets put the sound of birdsong in poems
it's a form of baby talk that gives me the creeps.
What do you think? *Chirr-reep, chirr-reep.*

Do you remember the well-known poet who used to wear
a chicken outfit? He wasn't advertising fast food.
He wasn't a school mascot. What was he? *Cock-a-doodle-do!*

There are all kinds of things to describe about birds
but to phonetisize their songs? Try writing the sound a hummingbird
makes trapped behind plastic stapled over a window.

One time a bird flew into a window and after a while got up.
(I've written a poem about it.) Another time a bird flew into a window
and broke its neck. I took its picture and then buried it.

*Hush little baby, don't say a word, Papa's going to buy you
a mockingbird* was a song I sang to my young sons endlessly.
And if that mockingbird won't sing, Papa's going to buy you a diamond ring.

And every time I sang it lines from Randall Jarrell's "The Mockingbird"
ran through my head, i.e., *A mockingbird can sound like anything.*
Or *The bats squeak: "Night is here"; the birds cheep: "Day is gone."*

Jarrell's birds speak Marianne Moore's *plain American which*
cats and dogs can read. Sometimes singing to my sons, I'd fall asleep
in the middle of a phrase and they would wake me mercilessly,

Papa, papa, sing! About birdsong, I'm not one to talk or,
for that matter, sing. And singing is something Wallace Stevens's
    blackbird
never does, not a note, not an *inflection* or *innuendo,* although in
    another poem

he says: *The birds are singing in the yellow patios* and *From oriole*
to crow, note the decline / In music and *For all his purple, the purple bird*
    must have /
Notes for his comfort. Poetry, Stevens told us, *is a finikin thing of air.*

Labyrinth

At the playground, a father was shaming his son,
and though it was none of my business, I made it my concern,
staring at the father until he stared back,
which was enough admonishment for me to turn away,

but as I did, I saw my son looking at his counterpart
who was looking at him, and in the stillness and silence
of their regard, the unbroken steadiness of their gaze,
they shared a recognition so complete, I didn't know
which father I was or whose son was mine.

The ground was made of shredded tires spread out around
a labyrinth of pressure-treated lumber. It had a "listening post"
where if you put your ear to its brass grill, you heard voices,
quiet and distant, but absolutely clear, and so near
one might tell you whose son was yours, which father you were.

My Mother of Invention

The needle goes up and down on my mother's Singer,
squat black with its gold scroll and script,
shaped like a smokestack turned on its side.

Have you ever seen a dipper bobbing in a stream?
It's like the Singer but so much slower. Its beak
makes thread of water and sews patterns of spreading ripples.

Such a fierce engine at the center of creation
and beautifully sculpted, a porcelain boot
or a falconer's gauntlet. The dipper likes the action

of a cataract, the rapid tumble of rapids,
and if it wants walks easily along the stream's pebbly bottom.
Hour after hour, my mother's fingers fed the fabric

through the pressing foot, kept the seams flat,
while thread spooled out and the bobbin coaxed up
from its metal gear held the stitch.

The American Dipper? What joy in finding such a bird.
Its short trills punctuated by sharp, clear *zeets*.
Its eyelid white against total gray, when it blinks.

If it didn't exist, you'd have to make it up.
You'd have to give it its own day of creation,
a day of translucent patterns, pinking shears, and pins.

You'd have to say, come see how the sewing machine
in its sleek skin dips and bobs and swims,
and how my mother, white eyelid lined blue,

sings her same stitched tune—never remembered
so never heard—and how like a solitary
calls out, not in air but under water.

Necrophoresis

The workers specialize according to their age.
At first they feed the queen her royal jelly
and then they nurse the larvae in their combs.
Some gorge themselves with nectar ferried
by the foragers and some offload the brightly
colored pollen to pack like pigment into cells.

As they mature they do the harder work
in search of blooming anything. Back and forth,
they go, back and forth, according to the language
of a dance, which also sends them to their deaths.

That's how it goes. And the queen herself gets
everything she needs as long as she makes brood,
and if she doesn't, if she slows and falters,
the mood inside the chambers alters and the colony
contrives a rival protected in a special cell.

In middle age, among the *domestiques* that tidy up
the combs, a few learn to carry out the dead.
Not a universal instinct, although almost all will stop
to lick the corpses, while others walk around or over,
tug or nudge the carcasses short distances and then give up,

but the persistent ones will shove the bodies
out the entrance to the landing board.
Sometimes that's far enough, and other times,
they're pushed into the littered grass below
or lifted in the air by others and flown off, not very far,
but far enough that when they're dropped they disappear.

Grandmother with Mink Stole,
Sky Harbor Airport, Phoenix, Arizona, 1959

It rode on her shoulders
flayed in its purposes of warmth and glamour.

Its head like a small dog's and its eyes
more sympathetic than my mother's eyes' kindness

which was vast. Four paws for good luck
but also tiny sandbags of mortification and ballast,

and in the black claws a hint of brooch or clasp.
Secured like that the head could loll and the teeth

in the snout's fixed grin was the clenched "Oh, shit!"
of road kill askew in the gutter. This she wore

no matter the weather and always, always,
when she stepped from the plane and paused,

at the top of the rolling stairs, she fit her hand
to her brow against the glare of concrete and desert,

not a white glove's soft salute but a visor
that brought us into focus. Mother and Father waving first,

then oldest to youngest, dressed in our Easter best,
we were prodded to greet her, she who gripped the hot,

gleaming rail, set her teeth in the mink's stiff grin,
and walked through the waterless, smokeless mirage between us.

She who wore the pelt, the helmet of blue hair
and came to us mint and camphor-scented, more strange

than her unvisited world of trees and seasons,
offering us two mouths, two sets of lips, two expressions:

the large, averted one we were meant to kiss and the other
small, pleading, that if we had the choice, we might choose.

At the End of a Ninetieth Summer

They drink their cocktails in the calm manner
of their middle years, while the dim lights
around the swimming pool make shadows
of that world they've almost fully entered.

Like Yeats's wild swans their uneven number
suggests at least one of them is no longer mated.
Added up, their several ages are short of a millennium.
This means the melting ice cubes are silent music beneath

their slow talk, and slow talk is how gods murmur
when eternity comes to an end.
The way it feels for these friends who amaze themselves
with what they remember—not the small details—

but how long ago lives happened and how fast.
Occasionally, usually from the wives, there's mention
of the War, as if they'd endured before waiting like this,
except now there's no uncertain homecoming,

no life to be beginning and nothing to complete
that doesn't wear already the aura of completion.
Listen, they are laughing. One eases himself up
to refill his drink. His wife, in a wheelchair, wants one, too.

Another makes a joke about making it a double
and gets up to help. They are gone so long,
or not long enough, that someone asks,
"Where's Bob and Jim?"

Now and then a tentacle of the robot vacuum
submerged in the pool breaches the surface,
squirts a welcome spray of water
then retracts where it continues its random sweeps,

until it breaks into the air again.
Bob and Jim are back, the drinks get passed,
even so Jim's wife asks, "Where did you go?"
Instead of answering, he raises his glass.

The Bees of Deir Kifa

The sun going down is lost in the gorge to the south,
lost in the rows of olive trees, light in the webs of their limbs.

This is the time when the thousands and thousands come home.
It is not the time for the keeper's veil and gloves,

not the time for stoking the smoker with pine needles.
It would be better to do that at midday, under a hot sun,

when the precincts are quieter; it would be better to disturb
few rather than many. At noon, the hives are like villages,

gates opened toward the sun or like small countries
carved from empires to keep the peace, each with its habits—

some ruled better by better queens, some frantic and uncertain,
some with drifting populations, others busy with robbing,

and even the wasps and hornets, the fierce invaders who have
    settled
among the natives, are involved in the ancient trades.

But now with the sun gone, the blue summer twilight
tinged with thyme and the silver underside of olive leaves

calm in the furrowed groves, darkening the white chunks
of limestone exposed in the tillage, the keeper in his vestments

squeezes the bellows of the smoker, blows a thin blue stream
into an entrance, loosens the top, like a box lid, and delivers more.

For a while, the hive cannot understand what it says to itself.
Now a single Babel presides in the alleys and passageways

and as block by block, the keeper takes his census,
he could go ungloved, unveiled, if it weren't for the unpacified,

the unconfused, returning, mouths gorged with nectar,
legs orange with pollen, landing, amassing, alerting the lulled

to scale their wax trellis or find the glove's worn thumb, the hood's
broken zipper and plant the eviscerating stinger.

The Concrete of Bint Jbeil

Pulverized is another way of thinking of travail
which is why dust rising midday from the streets
is white and burns your eyes and nose. Great machines
have done this to the mortar, block, and stone,
while smaller forces shovel rubble and rebuild.

Not far from here, south, in green valleys,
the realm of the better guarded has dust the color
of raw almonds, the kind its citizens eat happily
and call dessert or victory, but not with ease,
for dust drifts in scrolling clouds across their borders

obscuring what it will, and almonds unripe in their pods
aren't anything like dust. They lie in mounds near piles
of layered grape leaves, bristling with a sheen
of pale-green light so delicate you think the hand
that offers them is God's? But the hand is dark and swollen,

just like the one that bundles chamomile in tight bouquets,
whose small bright flowers are not the yellow of forgiveness
but the yellow that casts its shadow on the woman
who sells almonds, leaves, and flowers—the one
who makes an invitation with her hands,

a gesture with her covered head and sits for hours
on the ancient paving stones of Jerusalem, inside
Damascus Gate not far from Bint Jbeil or Dearborn,
in Lebanon and Michigan, where like everywhere, water
and cement mix with sand and gravel to make concrete.

Cyclops

My grandfather's right eye was a frozen slab
of milk-white ice that light never thawed
and when he slept, the lid didn't drown
the curse of its constant stare.

Look at it long and you'd be salt, stone—
fear's hard form. And look we did,
though we blinked against its spell, the worm
or ray or evil thread of its insistence.

I'd watch him read with half his face alive
and the other like a tool, oiled, hanging
from a hook as if you could take it in your hands
and make it work, but you couldn't.

The eye that saw the words counted money,
lit his pipe and bet on horses at the track.
It measured out his evening whiskey and led him
to the thresholds of our rooms to say good night.

O, calm, wheel-eyed giant, you might have tamed us
had we let you hold our hands the way
you wanted or stood beside you closer
when we looked into the sun and forced a smile.

But your hands were colder, more distant than
your gaze, and standing in our doorway your head
was like a moon, vast and disappearing,
occupied by all its phases, and so we tried

to pass unseen, unknown even as we sharpened
and heated the stake of our revulsion
and plotted when to thrust the smoldering tip
not into the eye that roved and guided

but into the one that monitored the smoky,
ice-stung realm inside your skull. Now that you're gone,
lift your curse, look at us more clearly
with whichever eye condones forgiveness.

Doctor Friendly

He was an example of anti-nominal determinism,
though he was friendly in manner, kindly
explaining that my light-headedness
and the cold nausea moving through me
probably, most likely, was the Novocain

he'd shot twice into a vein or vessel,
instead of numbing the surrounding nerves
and tissue—and that's why my heart was racing, too—
but he could try again, though only once more,
for that was all the dose a male my weight could handle.

Maybe, sitting in the chair, blinded by the watery
examination lamp, and still feeling the heavy weight
of the X-ray bib across my chest and abdomen,
I didn't have the distance I needed to make a good decision.
It was like the time I was thrown out the door

of my van on the second or third roll, and landing
somehow conscious but not unscathed in the road,
my only thought was to sit down, right where I was,
just for a moment, to collect myself, which is precisely
what I was doing when a passerby urged me to get up

and go with him to the shoulder of the road.
And that's what I did and that's what Doctor Friendly
should have done, suggested I lie calmly in the chair,
take a minute to compose myself, and then reschedule.
What idiot, blind, fearful, un-numbed part of me

assented to the third injection, I know well,
for who can refrain from administering
the shock or current, cinching the collar, or denouncing
the illiberal rule laid down for the liberal cause?
Who can concede to better judgment and be grateful

for the stranger who leads you from the road
and stays until the cops arrive,
or wave off the final swab of numbing gel,
that brought me to the brink again
beneath Doctor Friendly's masked, hovering face.

My Father's Knee

At ninety-two, my father's knee
is a harsh, dread spectacle
betrayed by Bermuda shorts.

Girdled in elastic, the cap,
collared like an eye, is blind
to everything but motion's pain

and this it sees so clearly
my father rarely moves
except to pee or shit or eat or sleep,

and sometimes even these
he can't negotiate, and yet
the shored-up knee is beautiful

in its boundary-stake refusal
to yield to the arthritic foot
that's ready for its shoe.

Wind

Don't return to your four corners.
Stay inside the lungs and thorax that once
released you to the world. Move in me,
so I can feel the pleasure of your passage.
I promise I won't plead for more.

As long as wind feels like it once felt,
as long as you are wind, I won't move.
Not even the leaves gathering at my feet,
nor their ravenous colors, are of interest,
just you, visible and audible, the pure

measure of yourself, shaping stillness.
That's why I'm standing here while you
are everywhere. That's why when I see you
advancing across the field, I won't know
if you've come to ravish or restrain me.

An Oracle

Choke off the wineskin's spout is what Apollo's oracle
tells Aegeus, king of Athens, when he goes looking
to cure his infertility, which was not the same advice
my neighbor Agnes O'Neill offered me
as I sat in her living room, watching her nurse her son,
who was nearly three, pushing his boy head
against her breasts that were flattened, come to think of it,
like wineskins. His knees pedaled her thighs
as he sucked and foraged, and an eye oculated the room
like the ego's manic periscope marking what was his from hers
and scrutinizing me as if I were foreign matter,
social debris navigated with cries and squirms,
while the TV shed its blare of light and sound.
And then like the casual, misdirected oracle I deserved,
she asked if I wore briefs or boxers
and before I could answer, she said, "Boxers,
that'll keep 'em loose and cool."
And that was all she said, all she needed to say,
as she shifted her angel child to her other breast
when he began to fuss.

Lashed to the Deck Rail

I'm glad now I didn't tell my mother,
after the urge to do so passed, the hundredth time
I throttled my teenage pecker and in despair,
and only half believing I had sinned, wanted to confess.

Such yearning and deferral, so much changing
of the subject of my inner thoughts, abusive
silence against the self that found its way to pleasure,
momentary, unfinicky, and followed by the utter, naked

foolishness of holding onto less than nothing, the way
"Mr. Boswell kept the deck" one gale-blown night,
secure, he thought, by lashing round his waist
a line a deckhand offered, but when the storm abated,

found it unsecured, the slack and flaccid
aftermath of such wind-lashed adventuring
held in his hand even as the packet hauling kelp
threw out its anchor in a quiet port.

And if "A Journey to the Western Islands of Scotland"
is too much onanistic veering, be glad
for what I didn't mention. The secret life of pleasure
is as dull as it is dulling, and no one loves himself

less than after loving to depletion.
But self-loathing is another story. Where did this begin?
O, yes, forgiveness. My mother as confessor.

Days in Paradise

The bird was on the wire and then it wasn't,
though the wire still stretched from pole to pole.

You saw it perched and still, except for the defensive
tilt of head, the tail feather flickering alert

and silhouetted through the setting sun.
You saw the sun set the eucalyptus trees on fire

and burn the land that once was sea.
You saw the sea in tides of dust and sand

that swept across dry fields and vacant lots
and in flocks of gulls and stranded pelicans.

You saw it in the cloudless days, the house trailers anchored in their
        parks
and palm trees, like massive tube worms, waving in the sky.

You saw its shadow sweep across the broad flat avenues
laid out in grids, in the bare mountains that ringed the valley,

the citrus groves bulldozed for houses. You smelled it
in the irrigation ditches and canals, the flooded playing fields

and golf courses. The bird was on the wire, the land
had once been sea: *Go ahead,* I urged my friend, who'd been showing off

his father's pellet gun and knew exactly what I meant.
Go ahead! It felt good to say the thing that needed saying,

to hear the barrel's *pfft* of air, to see the pistol's blur as it recoiled.
The wire stretched from pole to pole, the sun set everything on fire.

An Excerpt from *The Complete Catalog of Dogs*

The basset with its dragging ears and eyes like worn wheel bearings;
The Doberman with its prosecutor's tautness and preference for
    expensive whores;
The beagle's stooge tail;
The toy poodle's sloppy libido and two-legged embrace;
The mastiff whose tail whacks the swaddled baby Jesus from its crèche;
The wiener dog, more properly known as the dachshund;
And its countryman the German shepherd—black nose like a
    passport stamp;
And many more, i.e., the ink-spotted Dalmatian; the barrel-necklaced
    Saint Bernard;
The saddle-worn bulldog;
The frantic, dust-mop setters;
The eager, expectant, never-loved-enough, water-loving black-golden-
    chocolate labs—

    all of them trainable, more or less;
    protective, curious of scents, unashamed to squat or lift a leg;
    nosing park benches, bike racks, street signs;
    tracking squirrels and chipmunks;
    wanting to please;
    interested in the common stick or tennis ball;
    diggers of holes;
    shoe chewers, sock swallowers, book gnawers, food gobblers;
    haters of sirens;
    noble, conscionable, unconscionable;

shit eaters, butt sniffers, crouch probers, ass and ball lickers, tail
　　chasers;
farters, deep dreamers, barkers, howlers, whiners, criers, piddlers,
　　shitters

—and even this one, the perfumed Pekinese that can't escape its
　　questioning tail;
the shepherd's crook or crozier hanging over her like a bell above a
　　bakery door;
so many years she slept in an aunt's warped-open, dresser drawer,
　　she's her smell;
and when she breathes the tissue sheets she lay on make their papery,
　　emphysemic wheeze;
and her bug-eyes, O, don't say it, glaucous—black as a seer's.

Brendan's Hair

And we spent a long time hovering above the sky,
crying on its great canvas surface, tears collecting
in low spots, sagging the fabric through which
the sun usually poured. That's why we went back inside

and took up the brooms to push off the water and drain
the burden our sadness made, that's why we walked up
the aisle holding hands, straight to his white coffin—
a gift from the queen of cold and ice—and his white suit,

the touch of snow on the bruised forehead—icing
from the vault of death—and the white blanket
folded under his gleaming hands, and why we didn't linger
except to register the scalp, albino pink,

and hair in its last furrows but wrongly parted,
which is what my son wanted to know from that instant
of seeing his friend in the elaborate bed, he wanted to know:
"Why did they do that to Brendan's hair?"

An Amicable Breakup

I never cut out the eyes of her photos,
blackened her face, cut off arms,
stuck pins through her heart, the way
she did to mine and parceled them out
through the mail over weeks and months
after what I thought was our amicable breakup.

And I never X-Acto'd phrases from her letters,
pasting them as she did mine, to make
a litany of professions, underlined and circled,
with a fury I thought we'd settled.
                                        Oh, really?
Have I always been a stranger to myself?

When I ripped the sink from the bathroom wall,
who found the water main outside in the darkness
("Get away with the flashlight," I said. "Get away!")
then pried off the cover, and wrench in hand,
lay on the sidewalk, feeling for the valve?

And who rehung the sink, mopped up the floor?

"in his house by the wayside he entertained all comers"

You remember him, Axylos, son of Teuthras,
who lived outside the walls of Arisbe,
the one whose reluctance and humility
earned him bravery, who put aside
helmet and shield, broke the ash spear,
and begged we do the same,
and when we returned from battle
he sat with us and listened?

If we had been able to see through grief,
we might have guessed this man, "rich
in substance and a friend to all humanity," devout,
faithful to the gods, patient, unrevealing,
in time would absorb our horrors and join the slaughter,

and there meet Diomedes of the "great war cry,"
who sent him astride his horse, headless
to the underworld, blood drenched,
unrecognizable to friends and strangers he once fed.

History

When I met the famous *Felix Dzerzhinsky,*
he was a passenger ship and wore
a stiff, riveted smile as he rolled gracefully
over the eastern Pacific's long cold swells.
His head was square, like a stern, while his pigeon-toed feet
formed a bow, and his eyes, shaped like anchors,
moved up and down on chains.
You don't get made into a ship for being a nice man.
You don't become a statue in Lubyanka Square
without some "organized terror."
How else to build a reputation, lay the keel?

On a ship named for such a person,
there might be a man, in his sixties, bald, with a limp,
dressed in tweeds, accompanied by a younger,
much taller, elegant Japanese woman, a man with a name
that's hard to forget, who knows ancient Greek and Latin,
speaks French, Italian, Spanish, Japanese—his native German—
not to mention English in which you converse.
What makes him think the ship will never reach port,
that he can say the things he says about Russians and Jews?
Or that he can get through customs without opening
his big leather bag, right next to you, with its spare limb.

✤

A chessboard was painted on *Dzerzhinsky*'s back,
sand-weighted pieces as tall as five feet and easy
to move into position, but the passage was rough
through the Strait of Tsugaru: rooks, knights, bishops, queens,
and kings fell down and rolled on their pedestals,
like tops, while pawns upright slid around.

Who knows the fate of the U.S.S.R. *Felix Dzerzhinsky,*
perhaps it's a casino aground on the Aral Sea,
or like his socialist-realism sculpture, toppled by a crane.
How bad could he have been? I only knew him as a ship.
We parted after crossing Tokyo Bay under a bright sun,
although it was night in Yokohama, when we arrived,

wharf lights and cranes glared and hovered, and the tugs
that accompanied us nudged *Dzerzhinsky* in place.
Between hull and pier the lap of water was only
an expected sound, not a way of listening to the incessant
future shuttling between the present and the past, trapped
in a narrow channel too small for the ship I myself might be.

What kind of man travels the world with an extra leg?
When we said good-bye he gave me his calling card

> *Dr. Otto Karl Schmidt*
> *Osterwaldstr. 48*
> *D 8000 München 40*
> *Tel. 089/ 4 522 063*

and a folded piece of paper on which he'd written a request.
I've saved the Christmas card he sent in thanks.

On the front is a painting by a Hugo König,
Beim Türmer von St. Peter, a nineteenth-century scene:
two young girls, sisters, I suppose, stand behind
a head-high iron-work rail on a balcony. The older sister
wears gloves and holds onto the rail with one hand,
standing on half tiptoe, looking down—a city snowscape
with steep-pitched roofs and two church bell towers,
above which a flock of almost indistinct crows circles.
The younger sister, blond curls escaping from her winter bonnet,
looks into the sky, away from the city, or perhaps at a spire
that rises behind them. Unlike her sister, she wears
a woolen jacket, and as if dizzy from looking up so long,
her ungloved, left hand grips her sister's jumper.
(The grip is tight because Hönig painted
gathers on the fabric.) The scene must be so famous
most Germans, especially of a given age, would know
exactly what draws the younger girl's attention. Yes,
Saint Peter's tower, and the towers across the way,
patrolled by crows: the venerable Frauenkirche's.

Inside, a printed salutation reads:

Frohe / Weihnacten / und / ein gutes / neues Jahr

followed, in a tight neat hand:

Wishes you, dear Michael,
Your Transib-Companion, Otto Karl

and

. . . indeed you did me an enormous favor by digging up again
KRIVITSKY'S "WHY STALIN SHOT HIS GENERALS" and
I have been fascinated to read it over again forty years later!
Then I had shown it to Ambassador OTT in Tokyo because
I thought it was the truth, the German ambassador did not
believe in it. Now I know I was right. W. Krivitsky, alias
Samuel GINSBERG, a GPU-General sought asylum first
in France. Having escaped there 2 attempts on his life,
he retreated to Washington, where he was found shot in a
hotel on 10th Febr. 1941, two years after that article.

I would have sent parts 2 and 3 of Krivitsky's article
if his Christmas card had not included a Xerox of an excerpt
from *Hog Island and Other Essays* by James J. Martin, a
    Holocaust denier.
Even so, the decent thing to do was to carry out his favor.

And yet how hard would it have been for him to track down
Krivitsky? The articles ran in *The Saturday Evening Post.*
And Stalin's ruthlessness, he'd already detailed, along with Hitler's
opening of the Eastern Front "to save Europe from the Bolsheviks,"

never mind wolf packs off the coast of the Americas, nor his escape
from Dachau, where he was confined after the war—
this man whose motto was *Veritas est magna et praevalebit*—
and spent his retirement defending fascists like Leon Degrelle,

and publishing a book, *Pearl Harbor in neuer Sicht.*

❖

When I met the famous *Felix Dzerzhinsky,*
he was a ship on the cover of an Intourist brochure
and not the one I sailed on from Siberia to Japan.
The ship I sailed, the U.S.S.R. *Baikal,* was a lake,
and how a lake could be a ship, I don't understand,
and I don't understand Michael Collier, then or now,
who loves the idea that truth is great. He'll never be a ship or a lake.
He'll never have a cable cinched around his neck—never, never,
never!—pulled, head to pedestal, to the ground and cut up for
      scrap.
When he traveled the world in 1977, what was he thinking?
He wasn't. He was dreaming, like he is now—waking and sleeping,
watching himself throw Romanian lei from the window
of a train approaching the Russian border. He had more of it
than he could account for and was afraid.

❖

Before I met the U.S.S.R. *Baikal,* I took a train
from Bucharest to Moscow and from there
to Nahodka, Russia's Pacific port for foreigners.

In "soft class," the car's conductor brought us tea, morning
and afternoon, in glass cups with metal handles, sugar cubes,
and sweet crackers, that's all the comfort he'd been trained to give.

Otherwise he hectored us with gestures and disdained anyone
who boarded after Moscow. One night, he beckoned me
to his compartment. I knew four Russian words: "thank you,"
        "yes," "no," and "closed."

Everything was closed in that vast country, meaning "broken"—
"Za-groo-ta" is what it sounded like, and that night,
after many thimbles of vodka, I learned the word

for what it means to embrace the opposite of what you hate,
even if in essence it's just the same. "Hard-to-show" is what I heard
as he gave thumbs up to Pinochet, Baby Doc, and Franco,

and also, nodding to the corridor, where the man and his
tall companion stood, he repeated a word I didn't understand
until he took my pen and drew a swastika on his skin.

Memory of My Mother

The woman with the broom
in the turquoise-colored kitchen,
the woman who took two steps
and stopped before she swept the floor,
was not my mother yet.
She was just someone with three children,
married to a man not then my father.

A bobby pin glistens bronze
in a pile of crumbs and dirt.
How quickly things change!
"Me, Myself and I," the woman sings.

The sound of stiff bristles across the floor
is all I remember of when I wasn't—and she,
that woman who hadn't yet reached
for the dustpan, was someone
I was too young to recall.

Embrace

The great flowery dress of my seventh-grade teacher,
cotton or rayon, pillowcase for her vast
mothering bosom, scented with the perfume
of the unmarried, stretched over hips
that made arms of the lap I sat on—
you were the handkerchief of my remorse
just once, you with your bright roses and tulips,
spidery paths of vines and fluted leaves,
all the smothering penance that nearly consoled me,
until above my sobs I heard hers
and in her arms the crushing force
or the grateful fury of our unburdening
made that embrace a thing apart:
O heartsick woman! O bewildered boy!

Laelaps

When it was clear I would never catch her
and that she would never escape my pursuit,
Zeus intervened and turned each of us to stone.

No longer was ardor our fate. No longer
were days marked by bramble giving way to bog,
by razory reeds that cut our swift passing.

Days when all I saw of her was airborne,
arrowy—a silvery shimmer and flash of scut.
And gone, too, the late-night stillness

when I'd pause, not thinking to lose her,
but hoping, ahead of my silence,
she'd slow down and turning, see,

snout up, tongue lively, lightly panting,
undiscouraged, how at the edge of our distance
I stood, wishing she'd invite my approach.

But these are dog thoughts and I was god's
hound by way of Europa, Minos, and Procris,
so much passing on of love's troubles

I was meant to end. Who wouldn't want to die
into monumental stillness? Who wouldn't want
to be frozen in their last untaken step, translated,

like we were—my pointer's stance, her backward
glance—in the vast sky, where the gods below
had safely placed us?

Binding Spell

The helicopter on TV lifting from the White House lawn

reminds me of spells recited to freeze the kidnapper or thug,
rehearsed in the day-dream space of school dismissal

or across the open lots piled with tumbled sage
and repeated like a chant inside the mind's idea of itself,

words that brought the bully to his knees
or made the slowing Rambler or Studebaker,

—the driver rolling down his window—vanish.
What saved me was the curse that bound the object to its fate,

words that filled the urn or vial of dark wishes,
what once was etched on fragments of papyrus

lost for millennia but alive in calculations of revenge
or days of better fortune, and so:

I bind you, deceiver of the deceived.
I bind you by the tail of the snake, the mouth

of the crocodile, the horns of the ram, the poison
of the asp, the hair of the cat, and the penis of God

so that you may never destroy again those
you have invaded, nor call yourself liberator

you who have taken to binding others with the collar
and leash, while the dog, crazed but restrained,

yaps in the hooded face.

To a Horseshoe Crab

Strange arachnid, distant cousin
of deer ticks and potato bugs
those armored pellets
who live between bark and wood,
stone and dirt,
though unlike them you wash up
hapless on beaches,
more like a bowl than a shoe.

You come in squads
after mating in the waters
of your birth, dragging the useless scabbard
of your tail.

Often you die
still attached, fucked
but not fucking, though once
I watched the loved one
drag her expired lover in a circle
before she died, too.

And sometimes
in your death throes
you capsize on the sand, which means
you turn up not down
and your legs row at nothing
so for a while you keep the flies away
but not the merciless fleas.

Among School Children

The boy with barbed-wire tattoos braiding his biceps
won't listen to what his classmates say
about Yeats and "The Wild Swans at Coole,"
and when I try to mediate, he interrupts me,
not with words but with his lunging head,
half shaven, half in dreads,
the face unequivocal with rage,
and then the mouth's abhorrence,
lips pressing like a strangler's thumbs
choking the words he'd rather kill than say,
"Swans, fucking swans," as if he knows precisely
what they are: sleek, vicious, stand-ins
for the sad, divorced, abandoned
heart's longed-for wrong.

Danny Meyers

Fucking Danny Meyers, fucking, fucking, fucking, fucking
Danny Meyers, he hosed out a "gook" from the wheel well
of the transport he drove in Nam, and told us how.

With his piss and the steel-toe of a boot because that's all
the hose they give you in a place like Vietnam,
leather and urine, and the spit from the spigot

of his mouth. You think he's alive now? You think
after telling the story a thousand thousand times he'd stop?
It was a gook on a bike loaded down with all his shit,

pedaling away from his emptying village,
when he met Danny Meyers with his darkened
front tooth and his wispy combat beard and his

Fuck-me-fuck-you high-school diplomacy.
Fucking, fucking, fucking, fucking Danny Meyers.
You think he's alive now?

A Nautical Riddle

I was a ship but not on the sea

I had a keel unbuttressed by wrongs

Mouth and meridian   davit and hawser

I had a ratline draped forehead to ear

Billet and bollard   fo'c'sle and scuppers

I breathed in water, was keelhauled in air

Grog and bilge   hardtack and weevils

I was the saw that cut out the rot

I had seams that begged for oakum

I was the mop that swabbed the decks

And I was the swab

Vessel and fleet   harbor and berth

Week after week hammocked

Hammered and scraped   varnished and rigged

I was a compass fixed in its bearings

Coffer and locks   brightwork and windlass

I was a doctor with a briefer name   I was thirsty

Tell me, what am I   Repair me

The Singer

Soaped, dripping from ears to ankles,
scarred from throat to sternum,
like a seam fusing the earth's plates,
he stands in the locker room of the YMCA
and proclaims the weather in expletives,
scorns the bosomy widows in their flowery caps.

Dried, shaved, and talc'd, he grooms
his scalp, shakes out socks and underwear,
and then like the thing he most isn't
begins to sing: not songs, not tunes,
but the here and now fragments of fragments,
the *siss* and *sizz* of dentures, the chaff

and piffle of lips that almost whistle,
his arms flapping and flicking, throat
a wattle, feet claws. And what joy
in his strut, what angry magnificence
in his cherry-headed pud, red
as a thermometer's bulb in his briary groin.

Object to Be Destroyed

I loved the painter's ponytail
more than I loved her smears
and directed drippings, her grand
meanders of color that spread
in deltas to the floor
and left the ceiling pulsing.

I loved it more than when she crashed
my car on purpose
or hurled a trash can through
the kitchen window.
All those things her genius did
to make her genius bold and strange,

I loved, but more:
the sway, the plumb,
the elastic tie, the hank drawn tight,
its simple beckoning metronome
to which I fixed a pyramidal eye,
the equilateral of my regard,

looking back, and more,
following me, right to left,
yes directing no, give begging
take, now demanding never,
as if I had a choice to do
anything but raise my fist

and smash the gizmo
I had made, ready as it was
to respond each time I wound up
the unblinking stare
and hypnotized myself
with what I thought I loved.

Robbers

Bee-lines, silk-thread tracers not
tangling, not weaving air
but straight to the sweet scent
carried wind-blown up the valley.

Time's streak, time's lapsed contrails,
eye-level or higher, more and more
gathering, sun-warmed, sun-driven,
hoards and hoarded, divvied, scrumming—

one and one and one—by instinct
ravenous, thousands and thousands,
bobbing, probing the white stacked
hives, fragrant, humming—by infidel

or Saracen defended, whose fierce
difference are queens of their making.

Rabid head

so ponderous, it must be the problem he can't solve:
how to carry the bone-cage, the crash helmet for eyes,
and raccoon brain, how to keep the flange-like cheeks
aligned, nose working a proper snuffle

and the dark mask from slipping
or the tail's rings regulated and the black ink scribbling
a legible path from its fine claws, but here
on the side of the road, caught out in the light-storm of midday,

he seems to shake the glare of asphalt off his face
before he steps into the street—the heavy dowser
of his nose pulling his quaking, dithering body
near the mortal blur of traffic, and stopping

not to sniff or reconnoiter but to find the storm drain's iron mask
set into the curb and gutter through which he'll disappear.

Bikini

You might shudder again hearing the sound
of that word drifting down like a parachute
from the refrain of its harmless song,

covering you with its scant, cloth harness
and filling your seven-year-old mouth with sea salt,
kelp, and the coconut scent of bodies
sun bathing before your astonished eyes.

Yes, let it drift down, the top and bottom
of the bikini that is now only a song
so you can take up its tangle of unyielding knots,

and have more time to undo their fastenings,
more patience with their intractable dilemmas,
before you ask again those all-but-naked,
still-unreachable ones for help.

Six Lines for Louise Bogan

All that has tamed me I have learned to love
      and lost that wildness that was once beloved.

All that was loved I've learned to tame
      and lost the beloved that once was wild.

All that is wild is tamed by love—
      and the beloved (wildness) that once was loved.

Notes

"Binding Spell": Lines 15–18 are from *Curse Tablets and Binding Spells from the Ancient World*, edited by John G. Gager, Oxford University Press, 1992.

"In Certain Situations I'm Very Much Against Bird Song": Lines 17–18 quote Randall Jarrell's "The Mockingbird"; lines 19–20 quote Marianne Moore's "England"; line 24 quotes Wallace Stevens's "Thirteen Ways of Looking at a Blackbird"; and lines 24–27 quote Wallace Stevens's "Like Decorations in a Nigger Cemetery."

" 'in his house by the wayside he entertained all comers' ": The title as well as the quoted words and phrases in lines 10–11 and 14 are from *The Iliad of Homer*, translated by Richmond Lattimore, University of Chicago Press, 1951 and 1979.

Acknowledgments

I gratefully acknowledge the editors of the publications in which these poems first appeared.

Agenda: "Among School Children." *Chronicle of Higher Education: Arts & Academe:* "Laelaps." *The Kenyon Review:* "My Mother of Invention," "Rabid head," and "Wind." *Literary Imagination:* "An Amicable Breakup," "Lashed to the Deck Rail," "History," and "Piety." *New England Review:* "In Certain Situations I'm Very Much Against Birdsong." *Northwest Review:* "The Singer." *Orion:* "Days in Paradise." *Poetry:* "Six Lines for Louise Bogan." *Poetry Northwest:* "Binding Spell" and "My Father's Knee." *Ploughshares:* "At the End of a Ninetieth Summer" and "To a Horseshoe Crab." *Smartish Pace:* "Memory of My Mother" and "Object to Be Destroyed." *The Atlantic:* "Embrace." *The Virginia Quarterly Review:* "An Individual History," "Cyclops," "Doctor Friendly," "Necrophoresis," and "The Bees of Deir Kifa." *TriQuarterly:* "Grandmother with Mink Stole, Sky Harbor Airport, Phoenix, Arizona, 1959," and "Labyrinth."

"The Bees of Deir Kifa" appeared on Poetry Daily and in *Pushcart Prize Anthology,* 2010.

"An Individual History" was reprinted in *The Washington Post Book World* online and in *Best American Poetry, 2010.*

DEDICATIONS:

"At the End of a Ninetieth Summer," Robert and Lucy Collier;
"The Bees of Deir Kifa," Zein and Bilal El-amine; "Days in
Paradise," David Wyatt; "Doctor Friendly," Stanley Plumly;
"History," James Longenbach; "Laelaps," Judith Cloud; and
"Grandmother with Mink Stole, Sky Harbor Airport, Phoenix,
Arizona, 1959," Ellen Bryant Voigt.

Support from the University of Maryland Graduate School, the
Rockefeller Study Center at Bellagio, and Middlebury College
has been invaluable to the completion of this book as was
the support of friends and family. I'm grateful to David Baker,
Edward Hirsch, Patrick Philips, and Joshua Weiner for their
practical encouragements, and I'm deeply indebted to James
Longenbach, Stanley Plumly, and Tom Sleigh for their insightful
and patient help with this book, as well as to Janet Silver, Jill
Bialosky, and Alison Liss for their crucial attentions. Thanks to
Phil Levine for the pen. And Katherine, Robert, and David for
everything.